The Verse-ever Trip Around the UK

The Verse-ever Trip Around the UK

written with apologies by **Richard Myers**

Illustrated by Andrew Curran

Crown House Publishing Ltd
www.crownhouse.co.uk
www.crownhousepublishing.com

First published by

Crown House Publishing Ltd
Crown Buildings, Bancyfelin, Carmarthen, Wales, SA33 5ND, UK
www.crownhouse.co.uk

and

Crown House Publishing Company LLC
6 Trowbridge Drive, Suite 5, Bethel, CT 06801, USA
www.crownhousepublishing.com

First published 2010.

British Library Cataloguing-in-Publication Data
A catalogue entry for this book is available
from the British Library.

ISBN 978-184590441-8

LCCN 2010937283

Printed and bound in the UK by
Gomer Press, Llandysul

Crown House Publishing will be making a donation to Alzheimer's Society from the proceeds of this book.

Richard Myers is a bookseller, having worked for a number of companies, mainly in the academic sector before setting up his own company Books Education in 1997. His interests include comedy writing, most sporting activities, travelling, reading and music.

Illustrated by **Andrew Curran**, author and illustrator of *The Little Book of Big Stuff about the Brain* ISBN 978-184590085-4 and *Get Off the Sofa You Lazy Bastard* ISBN 978-184590445-6 and illustrator of *The Book of Thunks* ISBN 978-184590092-2.

In these somewhat troubled times
Make time to relax, enjoy some rhymes
We'll take you on a trip or eight
And help you to appreciate
The joys & delights of town & city
Even those which are pretty
Average. We've not neglected the local village
We haven't travelled to raid or pillage
We've included remote, unknown places
With all their airs and possible graces
We think you'll enjoy a different view –
See your places in a different hue
It's certainly not our aim or intention
To insult; merely give a mention
Of the pitfalls & woes that can ensue
Beware, dear reader, this could be YOU!!

I went to Aberdare
Where everyone gave me a stare
In surprise I averted my eyes
Shielding them from the glare.

I went to Aberdeen
A city so open and clean
Ecologically sound, even the granite
Is green.

I went to Abergavenny
Where the bankers were two a penny
But ask for a loan and you'll hear them moan
"Money? We haven't any!"

I went to Abertillery
Aboard the Isle of Wight ferry
Not an easy journey –
At times it got quite hairy.

I went to Ainderby
Steeple
Where ye shall reap all
Ye sow. Ergo
Populated by animals but no people.

I went to the Proms at the Albert Hall
Where the music did appal:
John Cage – left me in a rage
While Stockhausen I couldn't stand at all.

DO HURRY UP JAMES
YES DO. MY COURGETTES ARE COLD!
HARRUMPH!

I went to Alderley Edge
Where, behind their hedge
posh people live
eating their meat and ten veg.

I went to Altnabrae
Where for some reason I started to pray
I spotted a relic who proved to be the cleric
Saying kindly "Have a nice Dei."

I went to Arbroath
Nothing loath
But when I returned home
I'd a very mysterious growth.

I went to Armathwaite
Where I'd arranged a dinner date
Several courses later
I was extremely overweight.

I went to Ayr
For a dare
When I arrived
It wasn't there.

I went to Bagshot
Feeling a right clot
When I arrived
In my ocean-going yacht.

I went to Ballachulish
Feeling rather foolish
Wearing summer clothes
When weather somewhat coolish.

I went to Ballikinrain
To explore the wonderful terrain
I travelled by rail but sadly fell foul
of stranglers on the train.

I went to Barnard Castle
Where I broke a metatarsal
Playing too aggressively
Pass the parcel.

I started off for Barrow
But strayed off the straight and narrow
Don't know how
But I ended up in Jarrow.

I went into **Battle**
With a shrink from Seattle
Who claimed to solve problems
With just his **prattle**.

I went to *Beer Hackett*
Where I found it cost a packet
Just to play tennis:
Quite a racket.

I went to Berkeley Square
Where, polluting the air
The unpleasant sight
of the London derriere.

I went to Bicester
To see my sister
It was very foggy
So I missed her.

I went to Billingham

To collect my teeth, my dentist had been filling 'em
But when I got there his cupboard was bare
He'd sent them for whitening in Gillingham.

I went to Bolton Abbey

But forgot to tip the cabbie
Epithets flew, the air was blue
Frankly his attitude was crabby.

I went to Brasenose
A college in Oxford, as everyone knows
About a mile from the city centre
As the fly crows.

I WENT TO BRECHIN
MY FAMILY A' SEEKIN'
WE MET. TALKED ALL DAY AND NIGHT
RELATIVELY SPEAKING.

I went to **Brighton**
Arriving, I felt my senses heighten
Town out of food, sombre was the mood
And my belt I began to tighten.

I went to Brough
For the golf. But soon I'd had enough
The course was poor, scores of 80 or more
And not even a nice bit of rough.

I'M A NICE BIT OF ROUGH!

I went to **Broughton Mills**
The place, they said, **for thrills**
I pulled a lever and caught swine fever
And came home full of ills.

I went to Brynmawr
Where I ran into the town bore
He unfolded before me his whole life story
Blimey – did he love to jaw!

I went to tea at Buckingham Palace
Along with Bob, Carol, Ted and Alice
The Queen was gracious, but we were too voracious
So Philip kicked us out, but without malice.

I went to Bude
Met a Kentish girl so lewd
She cheated all she met
So was known as Miss Con Strood.

I went to **Caerphilly**
With my friend Willy
He got himself arrested
Silly Billy.

I went to Cannock Chase
For countryside, it was ace
Rabbits abounding, birdsong sounding
And not a hare out of place.

I went to Castle Cary
Which I found rather scary
Policemen in tights, reading you your rights
And the vicar, dressed as a fairy.

I went to Catchems Corner
To a funeral – I was the only mourner
Coffin into the ground with barely a sound
I'd never felt forlorner.

I took the ferry to Chale
With my girlfriend, Gail
We sailed a lot so bought a yacht
in a closing-down sail.

I went to Chester

So wet I wore a sou'wester

Off the Roman Walls I took several falls

Soon my wounds began to fester.

LIKE THE REST OF HIS CLOTHES AT ONE TIME IT HAD BEEN **VERY** FASHIONABLE.

I fled from Cheltenham to Dover
Took three days – I was a rover
Trying to forget my racecourse losses
Something I'd always Gloucs'd over.

I went to Chinnor
Invited to dinner
Nouvelle cuisine
I came out thinner.

I went to Chipping Ongar
To celebrate their twinning with Tonga
But – good grief! 'Twas TONNA in Neath
I couldn't have been much wronger.

I went to Churt
Very posh, very curt
Quickly left
Feelings hurt.

I went to Codda
Trip got odder and odder
Dinner served in church: pastor
Followed by canon fodder.

I went to Coed Morgan
Mistakenly insulting a Gorgon
When I left I found myself bereft
of a rather vital organ.

I went to Colne Rogers
Full of artful dodgers
And awkward old codgers.

I went to Colney
Where Orbison wrote "Only the Lonely"
What? You're sure? Oh, what a bore –
Another load of baloney.

I went to Colwyn Bay
(Bit of an away-day)
Bed and breakfasted on a farm
And the next day I made hay.

I went climbing in Compton Valence
So steep, I lost my balance
Rolling over and over, I ended up in Dover
Proving no limits to my talents.

I went to the Cornish Riviera
Where I very soon made an error
When a footballer I espied, and greeting cried
Actually wasn't Patrick Vieira.

I went to Crawley
Arrived feeling right poorly
Watched *Life on Mars* then to bed
Waking to The News, read by a young Sue Lawley.

I went to Crewkerne
To study economics – to listen and learn
A diligent student I was careful and prudent
And soon had money to burn.

I went to Cuffley
Walking toughly
'Cos I'd heard the locals
Treat strangers roughly.

THERE WAS SOMETHING ABOUT RUPERT THAT MADE HIS 'TOUGH-MAN' ACT LESS THAN CONVINCING.

We went across to Cumbria, to Staveley
Where the townsfolk regarded us gravely
Our hotel was haunted, but nothing daunted
We pressed on bravely.

I went to Cwmbach
But of humour found a lack
don't think I'll bother
To go back.

I went to Dalkeith
To lay a wreath
Accompanied by
My nephew and neath.

I landed by the River Dart
So hungry, I ate a horse à la cart
Not yet replete I decided to eat
A vinegar treacle, extremely tart.

I went to Datchet
Very soothing, nowhere to match it
The perfect place
To bury the hatchet.

I WENT TO DEPTFORD CREEK
INTENDING TO VISIT A BOUTIQUE
I KICKED A LOG WHICH TURNED OUT TO BE A DOG
AND BIT ME IN A FIT OF PEKE.

I went to Didcot
On the landscape: a blot
Could watch for hours the cooling towers
But otherwise ... not a lot.

DIDN'T CONSTABLE COVER THIS?

We went to Devon, hiking on the moors
Rained all day - damp soon filled our pores
Sheltered in some hay until gale blew it away
Leaving us clutching at straws.

I fled to Ebbw Vale
Having broken out of jail
Disguised as a baboon, then a raccoon
Thereby hangs a tail ...

I went to Edinburgh Zoo
Hoping some pandas to view
But "I'm verrrry sorry.
They're nae here, the noo."

I went to Elleric
Where I met the local cleric
Who told me his name was
Eric.

I went to Ely
Arriving, did a wheelie
They shook my hand and clapped, very apt
As they were incredibly touchy-feely.

I went to Faversham
Where the Vikings used to ravish 'em
More famous recently
As the birthplace of Miss Havisham.

I went to Fife
To get a life
And to my surprise
Found a wife.

My bro' and I went to Filey
With our girlfriends, Dannii and Kylie
Locals confused, then amused
Now they regard us quite highly.

I went to Folda
Got hit by a boulder
They say it's unlikely I'll live
To grow older.

I went to Fylde
Where the locals went wild
Simply when I ordered
A pint of bitter and mild.

I went to Gayleigh
For a ceilidh
Wrong information:
Should have been Rayleigh.

I went on a farming holiday to Gillingham
Spent all my days in fields, tilling 'em
I didn't get paid
So I'll be billing 'em.

I WENT TO GLEN URE
WHERE I THOUGHT THE WATER WAS PURE
I DRANK TWO LITRES THEN CURLED UP LIKE A FOETUS
APPARENTLY THERE'S NO CURE.

I went to Gumley
Hoping to meet Joanna Lumley
But she was in Nepal, having a ball
So I came home, glumly.

I went to Hamble-le-Rice
Half-price, so I went twice
Which was
Nice.

I went to Harlow
Singing along to Chris Farlowe
And, before I knew it
I'd arrived in Marlow.

I WENT TO HARWICH
FOR AN ARRANGED MARRIAGE
SAW MY BRIDE, SIX FEET WIDE
AND FLED IN A HORSE AND CARRIAGE.

I went to Hastigrow
Where, as you probably know
You can only use the toilet
If you pay as you go.

I went to Hay-on-Wye
Where the bookracks reached the sky
No time for carousing, just solid browsing
But still couldn't find a book to buy.

I went to Hayton's Bent
Found a field to pitch my tent
Plucked a thistle to wet my whistle
and breathed in heaven's scent.

I went climbing on Helvellyn
(Somewhat hillier than Welwyn)
Stupidly alone, I fell
And no one heard my yellin' ...

I went to Hitchin
Where I was itchin'
To see the birdwatchers
Do their twitchin'.

Seeking my beloved, I went to *Holmes Chapel*
Through the trees the sunlight did dapple
Then, with a cry I did her espy
Involved in a most unladylike grapple.

I went to Holmwrangle
Where my nerves began to jangle
It sounds absurd but couldn't understand a word
Our language they so did mangle.

I went to Holyhead
Looking for some lead
Fell off church roof
And ended up dead.

I WENT TO HOOK
ALL IT TOOK
WAS JUST
ONE LOOK.

I went to Hull
During a lull
Needn't have bothered –
Awfully dull.

Feeling guilty, I returned to Hull
During yet another lull
Place was bustling, people hustling
Earlier opinion void and null.

I went to Hundred Acres
Consisting mainly of bakers,
Estate agents and rock'n'rollers:
The local movers and shakers.

I went to Hyde
(Didn't really, I lied)
Just taking you
For a Ryde.

I went to Ibstock
Wearing my best party frock
Somewhat embarrassing
As I'm a big hairy Jock.

I went to the Isle of Bute
Where I'd heard the girls were cute
So true, I proposed after just one date
With hindsight, should have stayed mute.

I went to Jockey End
Into the landscape it did blend
So hard to find, I lost my mind
And couldn't out of here my way wend.

I went to Ilfracombe
Arrived with a sense of doom
Not helped when I found
A coffin in my room.

SAM WAS MORE THAN A LITTLE PUT OUT BY THE DECOR.

I went to Iona

Where I met Shona

Who'd only had

One previous owner.

I went to John o'Groats
Intent on sowing some oats
But the season was past – I was the last
Just me and a few wild goats.

I went to Jump
In the midst of a slump
Sights were few but a very fine view
Of the local council dump.

I WENT TO KEW
GOT STUCK IN A QUEUE
CRIED OUT IN FRUSTRATION
AS YOU DO …

I went to Kielder Water
Hoping to meet my daughter
But she'd already been and gone
Arriving before she oughtta.

I went to Kingston Lisle
In weather that was vile
Rained all day, roads washed away
So getting there took a while.

I went to *Kirkby Mallory*
To live there you need a good salary
People kind, but SO refined:
Eating nothing with more than one calorie.

We went to Kirkintilloch
It stands atop a hillock
Jack fell down and broke his crown
Silly pillock.

I went to Kirkton of Tough
Of which I couldn't get enough
Wonders galore, to see and explore
And a magic dragon called Puff.

I went to Knotty Ash
To tell some jokes and earn some cash
But some old bod by the name of Ken Dodd
Rendered my action somewhat rash.

I went reluctantly to Laleham
I simply couldn't fail 'em
Full of pains caused by the link with Staines
And a parking lot reminiscent of Salem.

I went to Lambourn
Needing a place to mourn
The love of my life (someone else's wife)
Had returned to her husband, Shaun.

I went to Leek
In a bid to seek
Spiritual enlightenment
From an old geek.

I went to Leicester Square
Where, out of thin air
I conjured up a hansom cab
Driver gave a very confused stare.

I went to Lewes
Via the canal known as Suez
Thanks to the chap with an out-of-date map;
He couldn't afford the newest.

I went to Lindisfarne
Where they love to sew and darn
There's not a lot to do there
But they certainly spin a good yarn.

I went to Liss
Investigating something amiss:
A stolen vase and a suspect from Berne
I was following a Ming and a Swiss.

I went to Liverpool
"Be brave, walk tall"
They said
"You'll have a ball."

IT WASN'T JUST HIS FASHION SENSE THAT MADE MIKE STAND OUT FROM THE CROWD

I went to London Colney
Riding on a pony
The reins I gave to a man in a cave
As parking for hermit holders only.

THE MIGHTY QUINN!

I went to Loch Fyne
With my trusty rod and line
Caught a kipper, NOT a nipper
On which ten people did dine.

I cycled from London to Land's End
To visit a long-lost friend
But she'd cast a clout 'ere May was out
Think that's a bridge I won't mend.

I went to the sea at Lowestoft
Where, in the air did waft
The stench of fish, and sailors
Up aloft.

I went to Luton
With my best suit on
To buy a bed
or perhaps a futon.

I went to Lytham St Annes
For a gathering of the clans
We partied hard until, like tubs of lard
We were fitted with gastric bands.

I went to Maida Vale
Where I partook of too much ale
Suffice to say the end result
Was behaviour beyond the pail.

I WENT TO MAIDSTONE
I WASN'T ALONE
I TOOK MY WIFE
AND SOME OLD CRONE.

BUT I THOUGHT SHE WAS YOUR MOTHER!
BUS STOP

I went to Market Deeping
Where I found the whole place sleeping:
Victims of Valium, I tried to rally 'em
To no avail. I lay down weeping.

DESPITE THE DIFFERENCE IN WEATHER THEY ALL THOUGHT THIS SIESTA THING WAS WELL WORTH A TRY.

I went to Marks Tey
Strolling through fields, trampling down hay
When I got into a row with a stupid cow
Who wouldn't let me have my way.

SOMETIMES MILDRED JUST WISHED THAT GEORGE WAS A MORE REASONABLE MAN

I went to Maidenhead
Where they'd promised a spread
A veritable feast, for five thousand at least
All in a garden shed.

I went to Mallaig
Seeking Henry Blofeld, arch-enemy of Daniel Craig
Blowers had wiped out MI5 and was wanted alive
To stand trial for war crimes in The Hague.

I went to Merthyr Tydfil
So quaint! They use pens made of quill
Bow Street Runners patrol the streets
Forerunners of the Old Bill.

I went to Midsomer
Proved a bit of a bummer
'Cos Midsomer's not there – exists only on air
so to go back would be even dumber.

I went to Milford Haven
Resembling Stratford-on-Avon
Without the Shakespeare
And of all culture shaven.

I went to Mold
Where, I'd been told,
They had a potion
To stop you getting old.

I went to Montrose
Arrived feeling very morose
Tried a bite but had no appetite
So I decided to stone the crows.

I went to Mount Hawke
Where I learned to walk
Not bad: at six months
I couldn't even talk.

I went to Mountain Ash
Where I committed quite a hash
In the town's finest restaurant
I ordered bangers and mash.

I went to Muirton of Ballochy
Where the terrain was extremely rocky
Imitating a stag, I slipped off a crag
That'll teach me to be cocky.

I went to the isle of Mull
Where life is never dull
Arriving just in time
For the annual tourist cull.

I played cricket at Mumbles
Slippery wicket, took plenty of tumbles
The cricket ball I couldn't hold at all
There sure were plenty of fumbles.

My wife and I went to Nairn
Made love in the shadow of a cairn
Nine months later
We had a bairn.

COR!
THE TOP

I went to Nether Wallop
Enjoyed a lovely dollop
Found a cosy nook, took out my book
And curled up with a Trollope.

I went to New Ridley
Just a little tiddly
Trying to sing like Elvis
But sounding like Bo Diddley.

I went to *Newby Wiske*
Shouldn't have taken the risk
For while walking around I was blown into the sound
By a wind that was quite brisk.

I went to Oaken
Where, strangely, no English was spoken
And by cannon shells, not church bells
The populace was awoken.

I went to Oakham
With sore feet, was told to soak 'em
In vinegar and brine they'd be just fine
What a load of hokum!

I went to the bridge of Orchy
Where they filmed the very first talky
Which is actually
a bit of a porky.

I strolled along by the Ouse
Where I ran into Tom Cruise
After a yard of ale he turned quite pale
Obviously couldn't handle the booze.

I went to Penrith
To dispel a myth:
An arrest for peeling oranges
Was merely taking the pith.

I went to Peterhead
Awoke in a hospital bed
Hadn't been rude, aggressive or lewd
So it must have been something I'd said.

I went to Pinner
To dine with Michael Winner
We met at the Kennel Club
And enjoyed a dog's dinner.

With my girlfriend to Plymouth Hoe
But Oh! What a tale of woe!
For after a tiff I jumped off a cliff
Badly bruising my toe.

I went for a spot of sailing at Polzeath
My arrival proving the kiss of death
Sea flat and calm, weather full of balm
And of wind – not a breath.

I went to Poole
Ran into a free-for-all
Banks handing out money? Funny
Ah! April 1st – April Fool!

With Billy Connolly, went to Prestatyn
But they wouldn't let us in
I was fine, got the thumbs-up sign
But they turned away the Big Yin.

PRESTATYN
DENIED ENTRAN : MEN WITH FUNNY
ACCENTS WEAR SKIRTS!
BY ORDER
DO NOT DARKEN!

I went to Portrush
Exited with a blush
Having been to the loo
And forgotten to flush.

We went to *Poulton-le-Fylde*
Into an old jalopy we pylde
Police were called by locals appalled
At our behaviour somewhat wylde.

I went to Quarley
I wasn't well, in fact quite poorly
I then collapsed, my sense of feeling lapsed
This could get no worse, surely?

I went to Quilquox
Where I experienced several shocks:
Don't wear a kilt when submerged in silt
And NEVER drink whisky on the rocks.

THEY WEREN'T MUCH BUT THE LOCALS WERE <u>SO</u> PROUD OF THEM.

I went to Rannock Station
The perfect location
for the head
Of the nation.

I went to Reading
For my wedding
Didn't last long
Divorce court heading.

I went to Redruth
Searching for the truth
Was it my drinking? Smoking? Flatulence?
Or was I merely uncouth?

I went to Rhyl
Where I had the thrill
Of my life. I met my wife:
Diamond Lil.

I went along to the Rhondda
Beautiful scenery encouraged me to wandda
Met Jane, a gorgeous girl
Of whom I grew fondda and fondda.

I went back to Cornwall, to Rock
Where I received a helluva shock
A Chinese meal with absolutely no appeal
All caused by a nasty piece of wok.

I went to Runswick Bay
Where I was faced with an amazing array
Of empty shops and houses:
Everyone had gone away.

I went on a pilgrimage to St Austell
Accompanied by an apostle
No room at the inn
So stayed at a hostel.

I went to the other St Ives
Where I met a beekeeper with seven wives
Selling honey but making little money
As he kept coming out in hives.

I went to Sark
(Where Noah built his Ark)
Working on Ark 2 I had a wonderful view
'Cos I was up with the lark.

I headed off for Scarborough
But ended up in Market Harborough
Courtesy of a dyslexic sat-nav:
A woman called Barbara.

I went to Scotch Corner
Renowned for its flora and fauna
Hottest day of the year.
Like being in a sauna.

We went to Seahouses
Wearing see-through blouses
Went as singles
Came home with spouses.

I drove to Sedgemoor
(off the M5, 2nd Floor)
Stayed above a police station
So I was above the law.

I went to Settle
To party, I was in fine fettle
And knocked out by the music:
Heavy Metal.

I went to Sevenoaks
Me and seven blokes
We were voted to sleep under canvass
For telling stupid jokes.

We wandered by *the Severn*
Got home around eleven
Glorious day – we made hay
And ended in Severnth heaven!

I went to Shanklin
To see *Aretha Franklin*
Though I could hear her, I couldn't get near her
So came back with bad memories rankling.

I went to Silbury Hill
With my good friends Jack and Jill
Jack fell down while Jill threw up
And I felt suddenly very ill.

I went to Skelwith Fold
Feeling extravagantly bold
Riding and hiking, gliding and biking
And I'm only three years old.

We ascended to Skye
With some bottles of rye
Drank from dawn to dusk
You bet our spirits were high.

I DROVE TOWARDS SLOUGH
STOPPING ON THE BROW
OF A HILL. SAW BETJEMAN'S FRIENDLY BOMB:
SLOUGH'S NOT THERE NOW.

I went to Spalding
With a view to hoarding
All their bulbs. Could be
Most rewarding!

I went to *Splott*
To buy some land – not a lot
But some old biddy outbid me
That's when *I lost the plot*.

I went to Staines
Covering my tracks, taking several trains
Needing to dispose of
Ill-gotten gains.

I WENT ON HOLIDAY TO STAITHE
WHERE I DECIDED TO GO FOR A BATHE
NOT A GOOD IDEA
AS I SWAM INTO A LATHE.

I went to Stansted
Should have stayed in bed
Went for some rest, some peace to ingest
Didn't bank on planes overhead.

I took a summer break in the vineyards of Stape
Thought it would be a jolly jape
Several bottles of wine, no longer felt fine
Had imbibed too much of the grape.

I went to Staplehurst
Feeling I'd been cursed
Having eaten a salami that eventually harmed me
And now I was fearing the wurst.

I went to Stirling
To partake of some curling
My stylist objected so I was ejected
Now a lawsuit is unfurling.

I went to Stoke
As a bit of a joke
Went as a girl
Came back as a bloke.

I went to Stonton Wyville
A village that has no ryville
The whole place turned out
Just to greet my arryville.

I set off for Stranraer
But didn't get far
realising, on the motorway
You need a car.

I went to Stroud
Found a noisy crowd
Waiting to see (as seen on TV)
Girls are loud.

Alice went to Sunderland
Expecting a winter wonderland
In mid-July? Oh dear,
Alice was in Blunderland.

*I made my way to **Sutton***
*Where I heard the **townsfolk tuttin'***
At my strange dress sense
Lamb dressed as mutton.

I went to Thames Ditton
Where I was savagely bitten
By a singer feline with a voice divine
An ex-Atomic Kitten.

I twitched my way to Thanet
To see a very rare gannet
Seen only once this century
It comes from another planet.

I went to **Thatcham**
Where the girls, well you couldn't match 'em
Witty and pretty, it was such a pity
That I simply couldn't catch 'em.

I went to **Thorpe Bassett**
Where I had to consider the facet
That, to be understood and the trip to be good
An interpreter would prove quite an asset.

I WENT TO TIPTREE
WHERE I MET GYPSY ROSE LEE
AND HER SISTER
ROSE HIP TEA.

I went to Tonypandy
Thought a dictionary might prove handy
No need! They all spoke Welsh
So all was fine and dandy.

I WENT TO **TOOTING BEC**
WHERE A **BOY STOOD ON A BURNING DECK**
HIS CLOTHES WERE ALIGHT - I COULD SENSE HIS PLIGHT
BUT COULD ONLY THINK **"WHAT THE HECK?"**

I went to Totton
Feeling extremely rotten
Staggered into a field
And *puked a bale of cotton.*

I went to Towcester
On a coaster
Shouldn't have believed
What it said on the poster.

I went with *Prince Charles* to Trafalgar Square
Feeling chipper and very debonair
Charles laughed at my joke, such a nice bloke
And in delight *I punched the heir*.

I went to Tredegar
Made famous by Pete Seeger
Where had all the flowers gone?
Floral displays looked pretty meagre.

I WENT TO TREFECCA
WITH MY GOOD FRIEND BORIS BECCA
WE TRAVELLED IN STYLE MANY A MILE
IN A LONDON DOUBLE-DECCA.

I went to the **River Trent**
Fishing for a **compliment**
No success and under duress
I packed up and **went**.

I went to Tring
In early spring
But the mist did persist
Couldn't see a ruddy thing.

I went to **Troon**
Laughing like a loon
Arrived before I'd departed
Got there far too soon.

I went with the lads to Uist
Fully expecting to get kissed
But girls found we none
So left looking at Scotch mist.

I went to *Ullswater*
Hoping to meet my daughter
Didn't expect to find her
In the Latin Quarter.

I went to *Upper Brailes*
Following the well-worn trails
Thirsty work so pub visit didn't shirk
Sadly, *I fell off the rails.*

We went across to Usk
And immediately started to busk
Locals said no, so takings were low
Dinner that night was just a rusk.

I went to Vellow
Feeling mellow
Met a joker:
Funny fellow.

I went to Venny Tedburn
The home of the Arctic Tern
And a vulture, but not much culture
At least, that I could discern.

I went to Veryan
With my daughter, Kerry Ann
And not, as I thought,
Mary Ann.

I went to *Venn Ottery*
Admission: six pieces of pottery
Which made getting in
Something of a lottery.

WELCOME TO
VENN_OTTERY
ADMISSION: 6 PIECES OF POTTERY
BREAK YOUR
POTTERY
HERE
(A FREE SERVICE)

I went to Vidlin
Getting time off took some fiddlin'
Overnight trip by train and ship
But scenery only fair to middlin'.

I went to Walton-on-the-Naze
Where Isaak spent many happy days
Fishing, and wishing
Hampton Court had a maze.

I went to Water Orton
But on entering found my self caught on
Barbed wire they'd erected (swine flu expected)
I felt the hairs on my neck tauten.

I went to *Watton-at-Stone*
Where I walked, all alone
Briskly up hill and down dale
Overtaken only by *a very mobile phone.*

I went to Weem
Where a beautiful girl gave me a delightful beam
We didn't tarry but agreed to marry
Then I awoke – it was only a dream.

I went to **Wembley**
International match to see
England 10 Finland 0
Finns ain't what they used to be.

I went to West Hallow
Where the countryside lay fallow
Little to do but admire the view
Then visit the next village, Marsh Mallow.

I went to West Milton
The home, I'd heard, of Dorset Stilton
But of factory no sign – 'twas the end of the line
The whole area had been built on.

I went to West Wittering
To and fro, townsfolk were flittering
At least, those who weren't busy
Twittering.

I sailed to Windermere
Overdid the local beer
Hallucinating, I thought I saw
On a mat, a pier.

I
AM
MAT

In summer I went to Wick
But came home in a tick
Too hot to walk or even talk
Even ice cream disappeared at a lick.

I went to Woking
Caught in a downpour, I was soaking
Squelched into a pub, asked for some grub
"FOOD??!! YOU MUST BE JOKING!!!"

I was partying in Wokingham
In every club was the only bloke in 'em
Danced with partners galore until my feet were sore
Spent all next day soaking 'em.

I WENT TO WOODRISING
WHICH WAS SOMEWHAT SURPRISING
BURIED IN DEEPEST NORFOLK
THEY DID NO ADVERTISING.

I went to Woolacombe
(Strangely, twinned with Khartoum)
Entering a church to pray I was turned away
And referred to the Temple of Doom.

I went to Worksop
But trip was a flop
When I tried to arrest
an undercover cop.

I TOOK A TOUR PARTY TO WREXHAM
CONFUSING IT WITH HEXHAM
OF HADRIAN'S WALL NO SIGN AT ALL
"MY GOD" I THOUGHT "THAT'LL VEX 'EM."

Down to Kent and across to Wye
Thought it time to give it a try
Met a mushroom farmer
He really was a fun gi.

I went to Yard
But my trip was sadly marred
When I fell out of bed and banged my head
Leaving me mentally scarred.

I went to Yateley
Which had changed greatly
Of course, I hadn't
Been there lately.

I went to Yelling
A property I'd heard they were selling
But price went sky high, leaving me high and dry
Disappointed, I could feel my tears welling.

I drove to York
But took a wrong fork
Ended up on a ferry
Welcome to Cork!

Back to York, planning some rambles
Stumbled into a thicket of brambles
Cut and sore, bleeding and raw
My walk turned into a shambles.

I went to Yiewsley
Not a place I visit, usually
Of places to dine, *nary a sign*
So I demolished a whole box of muesli.

IT WASNT MUCH AS ENTERTAINMENT BUT THEN IT WAS BETTER THAN NOTHING.